Found!

Reflections for Those Walking the Lonely Path of Pain

C. Kerry Smith

Parson's
Porch.

Found! Reflections for those Walking the Lonely Path of Pain
ISBN: Softcover 978-1-946478-26-9
Copyright © 2017 by C. Kerry Smith

All rights reserved. No part of this book may be reproduced or transmitted in any form or by any means, electronic or mechanical, including photocopying, recording, or by any information storage and retrieval system, without permission in writing from the publisher.

All art work pieces in the photographs have been created by the author, C. Kerry Smith.

To order additional copies of this book, contact:

Parson's Porch Books
1-423-475-7308
www.parsonsporch.com

Parson's Porch Books is an imprint of **Parson's Porch & Book Publishers** in Cleveland, Tennessee, which has double focus. We focus on the needs of creative writers who need a professional publisher to get their work to market, **&** we also focus on the needs of others by sharing our profits with those who struggle in poverty to meet their basic needs of food, clothing, shelter and safety.

Found!

Contents

Dedication 7

Preface 9

Introduction 11

Found 27

A Gentle Resting Place 30

Almost Can't See It 33

A Walk in the Smokey Mountains 36

An Anchor 40

Beaver Pond Woody 43

Completely Made 46

Creating What Is 49

Of Chronic Pain and Thanksgiving Dinner 51

Hands 57

Help! I Can't See My Face! 59

Just A Huge Task! 63

Listening to your Life 65

Me, Woody, and My God Forsaken Battle with Pain 69

My One Duck Limit 71

My Own Cross 77

Off the Beaten Path 81

Reflections of an Iris Farmer 84

Re-Stood 89

Still Struggling for Release 91

The Day the Lord Has Made? 93
The Gift.. 95
The Yoke and a Different Kind of Labor Day 100
What Do We Do with It? 106
What to Make of this Mess 108
Oh, Heck yeah, you ARE worth a lot! 112

Dedication

To my wife Karen, who has been by my side during this battle with pain;

Thank you and I love you more than words can say.

To my children, Jonathan and Allie who have been steadfast with their love even in the loss of a dad who wanted to do more;

I love you and am grateful for God's grace to you during this journey.

Preface

In the pages that follow, you will find the workings of my relationship with God as I battle Chronic Pain. Sometimes it is raw. Sometimes it is painful. Always it is with a view towards of figuring out how our loving God, in the midst of tremendous beauty that has been created by that God, allows illnesses such as pain. I have not figured anything out but in the words that follow, you will be able to crawl into my skin a little bit. You don't want to get inside any further than a little; it is awfully dangerous! My great hope is that this book will help you or your loved one who is struggling with pain.

Introduction

I suffer with Chronic pain. Like over 100 million adults, I live with a kind of pain that has no cure. Chronic pain for me began over 16 years ago just before Christmas of 2001. I attempted to pick up a Christmas tree that we had purchased at a local tree lot and throw it on top of our van and it had all gone badly. I am a big guy and strength is or was not something I was in need of. I have lifted dozens of Christmas trees over the years and thrown them into our vehicle for the journey home. I have cut trees down from Christmas Tree farms, picked them up, and carried them to be netted for the drive home. But this day would be different. At the very moment of this particular toss, a distinct pop occurred in my lower back unlike anything I had ever experienced. It would later be diagnosed as a ruptured disc in my lower back, and at the time of that popping sensation, I almost fell to the pavement. I never imagined how this event would be the start of what was about to unfold over the next 16 years: a life totally immersed with confounding, life altering, pain.

It has now been some 25 neurological procedures and surgeries later and I continue to hurt and nothing really has been solved accept that the government is taking steps even as I speak to limit the forms of treatment even for we who are justified for any treatment. There are few places of solace and pain relief in my life right now. You name it and I have tried it In order to get some kind of relief. Well, almost anything. Perhaps now my greatest struggle is with my mind and spirit as I wrestle with this constant, never ending, damned pain. It is a 24 hour a day search to find the help I need to live life and to find someone, other than my bride and children, to see through my pain and Few understand fully what the march through the corridors of a painful world entails unless you are in it.

I have lost much over the course of these 16 years. A career path in ministry where Karen and I have given our lives for caring for people has vanished. The diminishing use of my hands for my artistry that I had developed that gave directions towards a God of great beauty has greatly slowed. Mobility to be in the outdoors that I grew up loving and the only place where I could find a hidden God has become a work in futility. My own sanity at times has come to escape me. An extended family that would understand has at times been trying to my own soul. Financial security is now a question. A sense of purpose for the person God made me has required a work unlike any other. A farm that I worked to buy and bring to life has been lost now where I had plans to make it a place of rest and hopefulness.

Yet in this experience, something has risen out of this convoluted mess: I have discovered something deep within the recesses of my mind and soul that will not allow me to just quit. There is within me a desire to overcome this, this, whatever it is, this inner struggle that has left me with pain. Maybe all of this life has gathered to a place where my brain and soul have been conditioned to battle and overcome this pain. I even told Karen not so long ago, in a conversation about suicide of which I had contemplated, that the pieces of Kerry Smith were more important than none of Kerry Smith to her, to my world, and to my grown babies. I battle within my soul even that concept, the pieces of Kerry Smith being important enough to carry on, but for some reason, that whole struggle, a wrestler with the God of all creation, seems to be enough and at times, all that I have.

One doesn't have to go far in scripture to find those who wrestled and struggled with God. If you have come here within the pages of this book looking for some kind of a soothing relationship with the God you have learned and even partly created in your mind and life, well, this will not be that place. I am a Theomachian: A Wrestler with God. The terms that often describe God to me today seem all too mushy. I wrestle with God. The word Theomachy is derived in the Greek literature from the Greek Gods who would have a wrestling match, sometimes more than just a simple one on one. Sometimes it was an all-out Titanmachy where there were lots of Gods going at it. For me, in my own turmoil, I now find God, like Jacob found God at the river banks of the Jabbok, where I am wrestling with God.

The experiences of my own life have left me not with settled answers, but with a wrestling match that pits me against the eternal, not unlike the person of Jacob and his wrestling match with God as found within the book of Genesis. In the biblical story, Jacob sends his family along ahead of him to find his brother, whom he had stolen a blessing from, in order to get his own blessing from God. The story is found in Genesis of Jacob, just before the death of his father, stealing a blessing that would come from his brother, the first born of the family. It was understood that the first born would receive THE blessing as the patriarch passed into the next life. Well Jacob was the second born and he manipulated the situation and stole the birthright blessing from his brother and would spend years on the run, afraid for his life, believing that his brother Isaac would kill him. Fast forward now to the age of adulthood when Jacob and Isaac both have their own families and Jacob desires peace. Apparently, it had all eaten at him like life does to each of us and now, he searched for his own blessing.

None of this stolen birthright stuff would do any longer; he must have his very own blessing. So, when God doesn't just arbitrarily give him a blessing, what does he do? He challenges God for one of His BIG blessings. I'm guessing if you have the gall to demand a wrestling match with the creator of all of the entire world, you ought to demand quite a trophy! Not just stuff mind you. Not just more cows and more donkeys and more concubines. No, a big blessing; a purpose! A real life changing, life forging, generation to generation, blessing.

I'm not so sure if what Jacob got was what he was looking for, but by golly it sure worked. I believe that stealing the blessing from his brother had eaten at him for some time now, and he wanted his very own blessing. But being the second born, according to Jewish literature, left one without a blessing. Blessing. And Jacob had ripped off the blessing from his brother in order to be loved as what he understood being loved was all about, with cows and sheep and land and concubines and whatever else. Do you think that the stealing of that blessing, the hand on the head blessing from his blind father, the dishonesty, was enough to satisfy the soul of Jacob? If it had satisfied him then why on earth was he demanding another one, his very own blessing this time? And could this be the one thing, the one thing in our earthly existence, that all of life hinges on, a blessing?

Yet at Jacob's event, Jacob wanted more from God. And I think deep down so do we. So much so, as a matter of fact, that we will turn our lives into whatever we can, longing for that Blessing that we never got if we were raised in a dysfunctional family. We can fill it up with some things, but without that blessing from our parents, we will confuse our stuff that we attain with an actual unconditional, cheek hugging, body squeezing, life accepting blessing.

A Blessing. No word in the human language is more over used or misused or misunderstood or longed for or desired than a blessing. The writer of the song, "what the world needs now is love sweet love" is absolutely correct. And not just any love mind you; sweet love! Unconditional sweet love. The striving, the search, the longing, the acceptance, the forgiveness for all that we have done wrong, the hug around our necks, blessing! Oh, how our world searches and longs for blessing! A cheek hugging, body squeezing, hand holding, life accepting blessing.

I left my home in Georgia as a young adult and answered a "call" into vocational ministry and moved to college in a different state and found a home at Carson Newman College. A call. As in more than just a simple telephone call from God. It was heart piercing, life moving call from God that was moving me from my home in Georgia. Something was just amiss in the life I was living in my home. I felt so lost in my earthly family. It was not working and I found a little church who let me be on their softball team and I was hooked. I began to find some of what I didn't have in life in that church, in a pastor that loved me and people that could see me for all of the potential I possessed. I am convinced that in no small way, their love and support for me filled the void of blessing in some ways where my family never did.

I was the only one in my family to ever leave at the time and few in my family would understand. Well probably none would ever really understand. My call into ministry was just real clear and that same God who protected me thus far would give me the strength to leave a home filled with dysfunction. It was a tough, soul wrenching battle but I knew following God was what I needed to do and I had a deep-down understanding that God would never leave me.

Soon after leaving, I also discovered another hidden treasure that I had never comprehended could be buried in my personhood: Artistry. All of the experiences from the outdoors and my love for God as Creator came out in the form of creating something from nothing, mainly, carving a block of wood into a bird. While in college, I went to a gift shop in Gatlinburg, Tennessee and saw a carved duck. It was an amazing feat and I was hooked. I bought wood, books, tools, learned as much as I could, and it eventually blossomed into a carving business. I could use my hands and have a hobby at the same time of doing ministry. It gave me an outlet and I loved it. I entered carving competitions and won blue ribbons. At one point, I had 3 years' worth of commission orders. I owned aviaries filled with ducks and engulfed my mind with learning the anatomy of ducks and birds. I could reflect the wonderful creator God that I loved in my work. All of it, that is until; until the effects of chronic pain had made it increasingly difficult to do. And up until the point of my ruptured disc, God had done so many wonderful things and opened so many doors for Karen and I to make a difference. But over the course of the next 16 years, life had become exceedingly painful, and those open doors were slowly and more painfully closing, more spiritually painful than the chronic pain I was trying to manage. Even the ability to use the gift of my artistry was coming to an end and a deep, soulful, sadness engulfed me. Doors closed, relationships changed, limitations became livelihood, churches stopped calling, and one by one, the doors just slammed shut and along with the doors, the windows closed. I was losing a wrestling match with God and I was left empty.

By now, I had come to blame God for the whole entire mess of Chronic Pain! Whose fault could it be, accept the God who had directed me out of a dysfunctional system and through life until now, right? I was clearly convinced that this was God's fault that this all was happening. God had promised to walk with me and provide and open doors and it just was not happening any longer. How could God create such a mess of my life, abandoning me and leaving me as I hurt 24 hours a day, an opinion created in the echoes from my earthly father. What a mess he had created with his alcoholism! The dysfunction, the fear, the intimidation, the loneliness, how could God now allow one of His own chosen ones to fall apart like this I was lost, just as lost as I was in my earthly family. Call into ministry? Gone! Financial security? Gone! Artistry?

Gone! Friends and fellowship in a local church? Vanished! Family enjoyment, fun, laughter, gatherings, security, all now tempered by a path that would seem to have no purpose. So much loss for what I perceived as no purpose whatsoever! I was, in every sense of the word, lost!

As everything accept the love of Karen and my children were leaving me, so too were the hands that had come to create beautiful birds and art. I would awaken at night and shake them violently to get back the feeling. These strong hands that could crack a walnut, these muscular hands, were diminishing now. I had used them for carving and painting for 30 years and it had provided us with an income and some security. For me, it gave me a chance to create what I had seen years upon years in the outdoors through the medium of wood and bronze. But now I had started dropping objects along with being awoken with intense pain. They thought it was my neck, so I had cervical fusions. It persisted. So, I went and had a wonderful test where they shocked the ever-loving dung out of you which had revealed carpal tunnel syndrome. What was going on? My Masters of Divinity degree that I had earned didn't answer this. There were no answers to my many questions with the exception that, according to x-rays, CT scans, MRI's, I was now experiencing spinal degeneration and stenosis and arthritis and on and on. I came to conclude one thing: this was God's fault by golly! Opportunity was vanishing for me to survive. I was on a path that I had no idea why I was on. I didn't ask for it. I didn't deserve it. God had done this to me! Just like my drunken stupor of a father! It was Gods fault!

The results of the latest round of shocking tests was that I had carpal tunnel syndrome, and now, I could add that condition to my pale full of stuff. Good grief people, could it not stop? So, after consultation with my doctor I opted to have surgery to see if it would give me hands back. They would do one at a time so I had the right hand operated on first and, wouldn't you know it, it did not give me the desired outcome. The surgeon had said that some 90% of everyone that had this surgery received the outcome they desired. A "no-doubter", right? Wrong. I was in the 10% and I was now scheduled to have my left hand operated on. It had been 6 weeks and there was no improvement. None. I then debated if I was going through with my left hand even up until the final minutes before surgery. The night before the surgery, tears flowed like water over a waterfall. Years of accumulated pain, suffering, surgeries, and job loss had encapsulated and imprisoned me. The emotional lid was off and I let it out in buckets. None of it made sense to me. Watching my physical body fall apart was like the lumber jack who with each swing of his ax was chopping down a mighty oak, with my ongoing fight with pain being that lumber jack, and me, a mighty oak, strong, broad shoulders, good looking, well, broad shoulders, slowly with each swing, being reduced to saw dust.

After the meltdown, I made the difficult decision to go through with the surgery. Check in at the hospital was early the next morning and after arrival, I was prepped for surgery. I put on my cute little robe, and matching hat, and matching socks, laid down in the bed, and waited. I knew the routine. They would come in now, give me an IV, hook up the BP and heart rate monitors and I would be set. Surgery was going to be a breeze, right? I would surmise that this surgery was going to be a piece of cake compared to all those other surgeries. I was wrong. The first of a couple of unusual experiences happened to me on this morning. For the first time in all of my surgeries, I had a panic attack; a full-blown heart racing, high blood pressure panic attack. This was my first one ever. Karen was in the room with me and it scared her. Nurses came in, wringing their hands, and they called the surgeon who told them to administer to me a sedative. I was soon relaxed and after calming me down, I headed to surgery.

Surgery lasted only an hour and they rolled me back into my room where my wife Karen was waiting. I felt a sense of relief. As I awoke, I remember feeling no pain in my hands from the medication they had given me in surgery. I asked Karen for some ice and after crunching on a spoonful, something totally bizarre happened.

I must preface this by saying, I am not of the hyper spiritual ilk. As an analytical, over thinking Christian of sorts, I am pretty stale in terms of outward showings of my relationship with God. I consider myself introverted and thoughtful as it comes to spiritual stuff. So, the concept of a possible out of body experience just is foreign to me. All of the holy-roller stuff, I have not participated in. It's just not me. The only experience close to any unusual holy experience happened to me after I had made a decision to pursue a vocation in Christian ministry. At the time, I was the only one to leave my comfortable home and move on the faith that God wanted me to do something special. I remember having a family member to laugh in my face and ask me what was I going to do for money? I was just convinced God was going to provide. Why I don't have that same simple faith today, I haven't a clue. Maybe the stuff of life, all of the disappointments have left me stale and stuffy spiritually.

The night before I was to leave my home, some 35 plus years ago, I struggled. I remember sitting in my den, and really struggling about leaving the security of my life long home and something happened. It was a voice so clear that I wondered who was in the room with me. It was simply these 6 words; "I will be with you always!" I immediately had a feeling of comfort and knew clearly it was what I needed to do. This would give me the impetus to leave.

Those years since that time, Karen and I have indeed done some amazing things and at times I have forgotten those words and have felt alone and lost. But nothing like right now. It was a step beyond the loss of simple comfort. It was now the loss of meaning. It was the loss of purpose. Even the loss of calling that God had led me in. I had lost friends, financial means, and I just in no way sensed the presence of God. God may have told me that He would be with me always but now it was different. Or was it really?

Surgery lasted less than an hour and the doctors wheeled me into my room where Karen was waiting. We small talked about how the surgery had gone and I crunched on ice and sipped some sprite when it happened; I left my body and went and stood in a field. Gone. Not physically mind you. It was no near death experience. When I told my children what had happened, they wanted to know if I had flatlined! In some kind of spiritual sense, I left my body and went to a place where I had once felt great comfort in the place of a field.

Growing up, I used to love to hunt in fields of Johnson grass and briars and weeds. Rabbits and quail would be found in those fields and to me, those fields were magical. There was something comforting about those fields as well and even today, when I am able, I go and walk through those kinds of fields alone. Where family dysfunction ruled, Gods beautiful world comforted me. It was almost as if those tall grass fields would wrap around me like God's blanket, giving comfort when nothing else would. I remember walking through those fields as a teenager, shotgun in hand, touching the soft heads of the long brown Johnson grass, getting entangled in briars or wild vines, or being covered in beggar lice, the sticky little seeds that would cling to pants legs. I loved it even more when the wind would blow through the fields, making the Johnson grass wave back and forth, like the waves of the ocean. Sure, it was plain brown, but yet there was something comforting and secure about that grass.

But now, following surgery, following all of the pain, all of the unknowns, the disappointments, the tears, I spiritually left my body and was standing alone in a field. Yet this field was different. It was bathed in colors as vivid as any I had ever seen. Rich reds, vivid blues, brilliant yellows, orange brighter than the sun, all of the colors almost blinding were present. Here I stood in a field of long colorful shoots of grass waving and flowing from the gentle breeze that caressed my being. It was like the Johnson grass I hunted in, where I had felt comfort, but there was one exception: I felt lost and afraid!

So as I am standing in this field, I said to Karen who was sitting at the end of my bed, I am lost! It was as if I was communicating from this field back to an earthly world and she said to me, "what?" I repeated my words to her and said I am lost. I'm sure she thought the only "lostness" I was experiencing was as in a lost mind! But there I was, gone, vanished other than physically lying in a hospital bed, standing alone, in a field so beautiful it was almost blinding. And I felt alone and afraid.

The next thing that happened is something that I find myself continually going back to several years later. At the height of my anxiety and severe loneliness in that field, God appeared. I did not see God. I did not see any attributes that would relate to a physical body. In the Old Testament, Moses climbs to a mountain, sees a burning bush and proclaims that he had seen God. I am sure God is no burning bush. But something surely happened to Moses to the place where he could relate to others that he had seen God. I was now walking in that color bathed field, colors so vivid I could barely look at them, without a direction, without a way, and God appears next to me, takes me by the hand, and walks with me. I remember the great comfort I felt, now walking with God through that color splashed field. I remember the relief. It was as if, as if, in my lostness, I had been found and I felt the warmness of holding God's hand and the comfort knowing I was no longer alone. And yet, just as quickly as I got there, I woke up, totally conscious.

Karen was seated at the foot of my bed and I said to her, I have just seen my daddy, my God. Not my earthly daddy mind you but the very concept that Jesus related to God as

Abba, daddy, a term of endearment to God like a child's relationship to her or his dad. Karen literally jumped up from her chair, hurried to my bedside, stood next to my head and asked like a little child, "what did God look like?"

I started to cry. Not because of her question but because of the great comfort I had felt and now perhaps, the discomfort of being back in whatever faculties of my physical self remained. Like a baby, I cried. Yet too, it was as if in the midst of all of this pain, God had given me an anchor, something to hold me in place like a ship in the midst of this pounding storm. It was a gift unlike any other and now I was crying.

Karen wiped the tears from my face and I felt okay for the first time in a while. I did not receive any answers. I had no direction in life. I had no place to go that would provide for my family. My hands would not work accordingly and even now five years later and a number of surgeries, a lumbar fusion, two cervical fusions, a diagnosis of adhesive Arachnoiditis, additional hand surgeries and procedures, I still do not have my hands back to where I can use them as before and have been declared disabled. I suppose if someone could be declared disabled, 25 surgeries and procedures would be a qualifier!

I went home the same day as the surgery and given that surgery was on my left hand, Karen encouraged me to paint a picture of that experience with my partially functioning right hand, and with the pain still in place, I painted a picture of what I saw. That picture is the cover of this book titled Found! Because when I was lost, God came to me, in my pain and anxiety, in all of the questions, in the lostness of the pain of life, and found me.

Found

I came home, unable to hold anything with my left hand and painted with my right what I had seen. At first, I tried the good ole Sunday school edition of what I had seen and Karen, my wonderful partner and bride, told me in no uncertain terms that what I had painted, on this first attempt, was not what I had described as seeing to her. So, I painted over it and started again.

I closed my eyes and began to recall what I had seen and experienced just a few days earlier, and began to paint. The painting on the front of this book was what I saw. I have shown people the painting and even preached at a few churches with the painting on display and have allowed people to see for a moment what I saw. It is always interesting to hear what people see in the painting, things I had no clue were there nor had I intentionally painted.

Some see the spirit. Some see flames. Some see the trouble of my childhood and my struggle with my earthly family. Some see themselves.

I simply saw a field that I was standing in at the time, alone, frightened, yet there I was, in a field, a field with beautiful colors, only to suddenly be found by God. I then walked with that God, hand in hand, never seeing God's face, but claiming to have seen God, like Moses did when he saw the burning bush and declared he had seen God though that was no God he had seen, only a bush; that God. For the life of me, I do not to this day understand why I had that experience because frankly today, financially, physically, and spiritually, I/we are still struggling, still searching, still trying to know what it means to be "found!" Does one ever truly live their lives as being found by God?

I am not sure any of us do because, I think, the world would look a lot different, a lot more humble, a lot more graceful and grace-filled. About the time, we pull some pieces together and claim to have figured out something of the holy, we have to start over again, don't we? Whether it is through suffering, through death, through inescapable pain, through the myriad of unanswerables, finding oneself is a constant battle, a constant restarting of sorts. It is both a blessing and a curse for without that never-ending search to be found, to have answers regarding our life situation, we would never know Grace and Love and hope; would we? Karen calls me a gypsy soul, a wondering spirit, never settled. I lived in one place for 18 years growing up so one would think that I should not be continuing to wonder. But I do and my physical condition only provides the fertilizer to feed that wandering. I suffer every day with pain; chronic pain. I have had some 25 neurological procedures and surgeries and in the midst of that suffering, I cannot say I always feel close to God nor feel like I have been found for anything of good. I at times really feel absolutely nothing accept pain. Relief from this pain is always an exhausting adventure. This battle with chronic pain has turned me into a researching fool! I want to know why in the world some 100 million plus adults in our country and over 1 billion people in our world are suffering the way I am suffering. It makes no sense. And now, more and more laws are being passed that are limiting the kinds of pain medicine we are receiving rather than a strategy to find a cure for our damned pain.

The chapters and pages that follow reflect a number of things. It reflects my own struggle with pain. It reflects what studies and research has been done concerning our pain. It reflects my spiritual battles as well as my physical struggle. What I hope this book does is that it enlightens you to the ways suffering affects a soul, the person of Kerry Smith, and maybe draws you a little closer to God and helps your own struggle with humanness.

A Gentle Resting Place

This is the day that the Lord has made. But isn't every day? Our lives are not our own. We claim all kinds of stuff as ours including the actual breath that we breathe. It is not ours. It does not belong to us. We rent it. We rent the space between our ears, the space we walk on, the attitudes we express, the thoughts we think. We can rant and rave and yell and fuss but at the end of our days, we have a certain number of those days, preordained by the living

God and none of it, not one little iota of it, belongs to us. But we sure do think so, don't we? Enter the parable where Jesus talks about the wealthy farmer who was so satisfied with the status of his life that he built bigger barns to store his stuff in, only to die in the middle of the night. We may believe that we know and have a lot, but in an instant, it can all be taken away.

Yesterday, in my desire to do something less difficult than stomping around in a swamp, since it is the opening of duck hunting season, I decided to do something less strenuous like bow hunting for deer, which I have little confidence in and little previous success. Oh don't fear, Bambi would be safe and besides, I needed something to protect me from marauding bands of squirrels that may try to chew my leg into a nub.

Unable to climb into a tree and looking for a place to sit, while walking through the woods in the predawn darkness, already in pain and hoping that this precious time would help to alleviate some of the stress of my journey with pain, I fell. Yep, landing gear up and in slow motion, I landed; touchdown! Only the landing strip was right on my crossbow! Not sure what all the cracking was upon my graceful landing, but as sore as I am today, I think it was at least some of me. I think my crossbow got it too though I won't know until later today. Believe me, the killing of something was not at the forefront of my noggin to start with; it was the fact that I could go outside and meld into the life of the natural world. Oh, I melded alright, right into the freshly made mud from our latest storm. It has left me sore. It has left me realizing something else; our life just is not our own!

An owl let out a string of hoots that sounded more like a deep, hysterical belly laugh. I think I was the object of his sickly joke. The crows found him right after daylight and made a mockery of his attempts to hide, telling everyone within miles of earshot of his potential murderous desires. The wood ducks flew and squealed in their excitement for finding a few acorns in the swamp that I inhabited. The mallards quacked and chuckled, circling and looking for a place to land for their early morning breakfast. The robins awoke, chirping with the acknowledgement that an invader was present. And in the world I now occupied, I realized, no matter how much I have gone through and am going through, I was small. I was a simple little piece of a bigger puzzle that was around me.

I would never think that what I go through as a curse by God. It has been a journey of questions with no answers, of denial and acceptance, of frustration and disappointment. For each of us, in our attempt to control everything that scares us to death, suffering comes to us. But do you know what else it is? This damnable pain is a gift! It is a gift where the model of my existence has been pulled apart like a box of Legos and is being reassembled into something different.

What that is, I haven't a clue but one thing I do know; I realize that the footprints of my existence on this rotating rock is small and is only made relevant by acknowledging the presence of a God that walks with us in the midst of our suffering and pain. I may have cracked my bow. I probably cracked my spine. I definitely am reminded that in our imperfections and suffering, God is as close as the laughing owl and barking squirrel.

Almost Can't See It

My latest carving project is this little hummingbird pictured above. It gets smaller as I carve it down to what I believe it to be the actual size of these special birds. We have a trumpet vine that is draped around our arbor and after almost getting skewered by one of the little speed demons at about dawn this morning, I got to thinking, which has proven lately to be a dangerous event. Make no mistake about it, these tiny dudes and dudettes, weighing about the same amount of a penny, are serious!

So yesterday, I pulled up a stool, grabbed the floor mic at the East Acres Baptist Church, on the day that the Lord had made, and proclaimed the word. I would dare say that Jesus neither used a stool nor floor mike. I am sure however that in some form or fashion he did have a story regarding brokenness; broken families, broken religion, broken lives, and broken beliefs. He talked about a seed one day, a tiny seed that by itself, had not a bit of significance. But put a little manure in there with that speck of a seed and a little soil and maybe a rotten fish or two, and there, right there, maybe something would take root and sprout and grow and become a plant of significance and purpose.

I am not sure anything related to my own journey with pain is small or worthwhile in a vacuum. Leave it alone and it will pretty near eat a person alive! You talk to any of us out here where this stuff "aggrabates"(Allies word when she was little and Jonathan was bugging her) us and it starts to sound like a broken record. Try to find something that helps, and guess what, it doesn't and understanding for our situation becomes fuzzy, a stress of where it all ends or how, creating the fear of the unknown, sadness, financial worry, oh wow, it goes on and on.

None of us though can pick and choose or should I say, should pick and choose what parts of the Bible we hold on to or believe more strongly than other parts, than we can pick and choose the stuff that will beset our very circumstances. We think we have control but alas, we really don't! All of us. Healthy and unhealthy, we are far more similar than different, no matter what you may think. Which makes this whole concept of a tiny little mustard seed quite unique. A mustard seed is as close to nothing as a little germ or a flea. You have to squint your eyes to even see it. Heck, I would just about go plum blind trying to see the little bits, like it will be when I put eyes in this little hummingbird carving. But that seed IS there. Right there

Found!

in front of your eyes only one almost needs a magnifying glass to see it, like I am using with my little hummer!

I don't fully understand a lot; heck, probably very little and certainly almost nothing about my own predicament. As I preached the word yesterday, sitting on a stool, massaging my legs because lord knows they were sure hurting, I kept thinking as I spoke; Can my small words, words that echo in the chambers of people who suffer, make a difference, even while I sit here and suffer? Can, in the midst of this difficulty, I grasp something worth grasping, in the life giving event of associating with others who hurt, even, yea, while I am hurting myself? Can I embrace a tiny seed of hope and plant it somewhere, somewhere with some people who they too yet struggle and hurt and rub their own legs while doing whatever they have to? I would just as soon not. I would. Put me back in coach, I am ready to play today! But it's not happening. It is only a seed.

A Walk in the Smokey Mountains

It wasn't just any walk. It was a moderate hike, as grading systems go, according to our son. We didn't hear him though and, what's that word again that is used, a…ass….umed, that's it, ASSUMED it would be an easy hike. Were we ever wrong! The thought never crossed our minds to turn back. We were so ill equipped for the HIKE, yes it was a HIKE, and we had nothing accept the clothes on our back. Bad shoes, light weight coat, but it was warm down where we were. But we were not going to stay 'where we were'!

The hike was almost 6 miles according to the sign. It turned out to be 7. It consisted of over 17,000 steps, 17,000!!!! steps of a slow uphill grade that was supposed to allow us to be at the base of a waterfall which was actually a little tiny drip. It was over, get this, 140 floors like you were climbing up the steps of a building. 140!!!!!

What was happening to me now, was that the myriad of medications and supplements, as recommended by the only doctor diagnosing people with Adhesive Arachnoiditis, as well as the use of magnets to help manage my pain, were allowing me to walk. But I will say right here, there is no supplement that can help stupidity and this was STUPID! I told my pain doctor about this hike and he said, "Congratulations now DO NOT DO THIS EVER AGAIN!!!!"

If you are struggling with pain, you do and have to do some stupid stuff, stuff that you once did with a healthy back but now can't do quite as much as you once did, but still, it is stupid to do if you suffer with chronic pain, AND this was stupid. A hike up a mountain where the temperature dropped from 57 to 38 degrees with snow and we had no coat, no snacks, NO NOTHING!!! And after viewing what was supposed to be a waterfall, we headed back down the mountain, having picked up some walking sticks to help us crawl down the mountain, where after a total of 6 hours, we found my truck. Never have seats felt so comfortable and oranges tasted so good.

The great thing about this was that I was not hurting, thankfully from magnetic support in my lower back, as much as I thought I would. Oh it was fantastic but I paid for it, but not badly. One question for we who suffer with pain is how much living can we actually do? How can we live life while we struggle knowing that what we do will cause us pain? And the issue of acceptance fits perfectly into our way of thinking right at this point.

Once we accept what we have, then we are able to prepare for our days, unless we do something STUPID like I did, but still, by accepting our pain, knowing there may never be a cure for it, we can face our issues.

Last Christmas I painted a picture for Karen that is included in this blog post. It has a big, strong oak tree that is located next to the road and inside of a special place called Cades Cove in the Smokey Mountains. The tree stands tall and strong and alone. There are mountains all around, fences that used to corral cattle, the regular low lying clouds that are a part of this place, and a road that goes right by that strong old Oak tree.

The tree represents what I would like to be which is strong, strong enough to weather storms that life is hurling at me and my family, strong enough to absorb the storms that me and my family face daily. The same thing is for you I'm sure if you suffer with chronic pain. The road in the picture represents how life continues with people driving by, taking the tree for granted, not stopping to climb into its limbs or to wrap their arms around it to just say thanks for the beauty you possess and the strength. But you know what? That tree is strong, just like you and me.

The road may travel next to you with people for the most part never totally understanding this lonely path you are on. But there you are; strong, wind, hail, and rain proven, strong. You may not be able to do what you once did, but there sure are things that you can do and living your life, as best you know how means that you and I are indeed strong.

If people live long enough, they will encounter suffering. All of us will and perhaps that is where you are now struggling to survive. Remember one thing; the suffering we have encountered, the lonely struggle that we find ourselves in, has made us strong. I don't like it. I don't like it one bit and wish I didn't have to go through this pain. But what I show the world around me is that I can still love my family and emotionally support them and help them to become, like the lightly colored orange trees that you see in the picture, strong oak trees, able to withstand the stuff that life throws at them, the wind, the rain, the hail, the storms just like me and just like you.

God is present in our suffering, helping us to stand as the Oak Tree stands in the picture. More days than not, I do not feel the presence of God in anything. More days than not, I suffer and do not think of God. Yet, unbeknownst to us, scripture teaches us that God walks with us in our suffering. Scripture tells us that there is no place we can go without God being there. Like the roots to that old Oak Tree, God holds us to face the storms, even when we don't see it or feel it.

An Anchor

The opening narrows over time. The interest slowly comes to an end. The emails, phone calls, and notes, all slowly dry up. People live busy lives. And nothing in our busy life changes accept the resolve that what is, is. There is no late night commercial that shows pictures of us. And maybe if you ever saw us, you would say," gosh, how very good you look!" And we don't complain because all the complaining that we can muster is of no use. And in the darkness, in the midst of the storm that never ends, it is there, if for no other reason than because, it's who we are; we are a hoping people! At the end of all of us, whether your condition is chronic with pain, or not, nothing defines our real worth accept for one thing; our hope.

I love my shop! I go out and create in it, hoping to make something even more beautiful than the last object of my affection. But it is not the same now. It is an illusion of what was. Very little of my creative self works as it should or did and many days I walk out of that shop feeling more frustrated and in pain than creative and fulfilled. My neck pops and grabs. My hands freeze up and require me to stop and massage them. My back and legs begin to ache and I stand and walk around, often interrupting a creative thought or moment. Even yesterday, my anniversary day, I underwent more tests to see why all of my pain has now reoccurred. And yet, as they say, it is what it is! And to accept this as such is not in my DNA! I push every envelope possible! Ask Karen Castle Smith!

I challenge the boundaries of what is, all the way and up to, what can be! And if I am not careful, this mantra of my existence can be the anchor of my future. And only when the pain comes searing through the parts that are creative, do I stop and process it all and realize this one fact; my ability to create is not the anchor of my being. The anchor of my being is on one simple truth: It ain't over til it's over! Our foundation, our anchor is found not on one of any of the above qualifiers to our personhood. Our anchor is found only on that which we didn't have a bit to do with. Our anchor is found on the very essence of our faith; a belief and hope that our life here is not all there is! And I have to remind myself of this as my body continues to do whatever it is that it is going to do.

For centuries, anchors have been a symbol of hope. This emblem was especially significant to the early persecuted church. Many etchings of anchors were discovered in the catacombs of Rome, where Christians held their meetings in hiding. Threatened with death because of their faith,

Christians used the anchor as a disguised cross and as a marker to guide the way to their secret meetings.

My ability to carve may become diminished. I may have to change the way I do what I love and that may stop altogether. Churches and Institutions have misunderstood the physical dynamic that has come to define too much of my existence and have judged me accordingly. And incorrectly may I add! But my anchor and hope is not on my stuff, my abilities, my inabilities, my gifts, nor my talents. My anchor is found in the hope of a new day that will dawn because of my faith.

Beaver Pond Woody

The clay pot is sealed and buried in the middle of the beaten down clay dirt floor. It is all they have. There is no bank to invest it in. There is no portfolio, no 401K. It is all they have and they pray they will not need it anytime soon. But they know if they need it, they can access it, digging it up, and breaking the clay pot that it resides in.

I am not sure if anyone has ever done a "gospel according to the clay pot that houses the family treasure." What would it say if it could talk? Perhaps it would say, "My greatest purpose is not yet realized! I will have to be busted and broken for you to get at what I am holding!" Maybe it would echo, "I am made by the hands of a great potter, as are you, and my purpose will never be realized until I am broken, just like you." But there is that inference right there in the holy writ. Paul talked about it as he dealt with his own brokenness. It was as if he understood that to be fully human and fully purposeful it is realized only when we are broken.

It is a novel concept, isn't it? In a society of hunks and hormones, of strength and stamina, we are given the illustration by Paul that we are a pot, formed by a great potter, and that found inside of us is a treasure, which is released and given by only being broken. Unexpected illness, unexplained death, hopes destroyed, grieving, heart-wrenching, cancer filled; broken!

It is T-minus 11 days and I pray I have done this special art piece the justice it deserves. It will be surrounded at the time of its presentation by hundreds of art pieces that have been completed by artists whose health was in no way compromised and they were able to spend months and years on some of them, concentrating with no distractions, each stroke of the hand having nothing in the way but his or her own imagination. I will be compared to each of them accordingly with so few having a faint clue to the person behind the creation of this flying wood duck that I have called, "Beaver Pond Woody".

I have yet to know why in the world I chose to do of all ducks, a flying one and on top of that, the most colorful of all ducks, all complicated with the fact that the artist doing this piece is "all broke up." My day begins by placing my brain in gear for the pain that will momentarily run throughout my body. Bed is my good friend and enemy, all wrapped up in one. I start by massaging my hands, rubbing my neck, massaging my back, trying to get up enough strength to stand, grabbing door facings, an ironing board, anything that will help me to start. Each breath and every

Found!

heartbeat shoots a signal to my brain that I am not at my best because I am broken.

I think of the work that lies before me for this day. I think of my children where each day brings their own set of stressors and I think about the person God has given me to walk with, in the midst of it all and I pray. For all that I don't understand and all that awaits and the reasoning beyond my own understanding of pain and suffering, I stop and pray for one thing: that the treasure that is found inside of this broken pot will be of value to the brokenness of our own world.

Completely Made

Look at em all sitting there, all those decoys, ready to be completed. Right now it is 4:30 in the danged morning and I am hurting like a son of a gun. (Cleaned that one up, eh?) I started physical therapy last week from my 7 month old fusion surgery and I am hurting immensely this morning. Physical it definitely is; therapy the book is still out on! But I am also hurting emotionally and spiritually this morning because of the emotional and spiritual pain that friends and family are going through. In this pain, this God forsaken wrath of pain, I have come to understand one thing clearly: We are made complete through our pain and suffering!

Little did I know that the creations of these decoys, of all my art work, would contribute to the pain I am in. I gave Karen a decoy years ago and I call it my pain duck because

I would lie in bed and carve the duck in between surgeries and procedures. My carvings, all of them are connected to me because of my own pain and the only way these decoys pictured above or any art piece will be complete is to work through my own pain and complete them. All of it, every smidgen of the art I do, is made complete out of my own pain and suffering.

When Karen and I lived in Montana almost 30 years ago and I was pastoring the little church we had started, a friend of mine and myself would meet every Wednesday morning and memorize scripture and pray together. The book we memorized was the book of James. I have since forgotten most of it with the exception of one passage which is the actual beginning of the book:

"James, a bond servant of The Lord Jesus Christ, to the twelve tribes scattered abroad, greetings! Consider it all joy my brethren (and sistren may I add) when you encounter various trials, knowing that the testing of your faith produces endurance. And let endurance have its perfect result that you may be perfect and complete, lacking in nothing."

Really? All this suffering that we go through making us perfect? Okay already, I'm about as perfect as I would like to be doggone it! This, my friends, will be a topic of intense discussion when I see God someday. This whole suffering deal and even Jesus suffering on the cross; really and why? One purpose to all of this suffering is that others are made complete because of our own pain and suffering.

We are made complete, our faith is made complete because of the suffering of Christ and our own suffering because in no other way, no other way, do we experience the fullness of God. "And let endurance have its perfect result, that you (me, us) may be perfect and complete, lacking in nothing!

This is the world we live in. We will not get out of here unscathed. All of us will be and are bruised and battered. The fullness of God is made complete in suffering. My carvings, my own creations, my decoys, my birds, are made complete, knife in hand, struggling all around, the grain of the wood, the push and the pull, the chips that fly and the clouds of dust, those art pieces are made complete in my own pain and suffering. And so too is our faith

Creating What Is

The stuff that we portray and copy and assume about life can all change one day, and we spend the rest of our existence trying to figure it all out again. That's the beauty of being an artist. We can work from a picture, like the carving and burning of a Cooper's Hawk tail that I once did. What is, can be changed or recreated to what should be. Until, well, until.

One day, it gets turned upside down and the artwork has become you and you get up, dust yourself off, and watch as other people forget you accept your family and your God, of which by the way, you hope not and yet try to figure out where or what or who that God is found to be.

The institutional church, rightly and wrongly holds on to what was and struggles with what could be. And those of us, outside of that institution because of a curse, or maybe, just maybe, a blessing, stand up, dust ourselves off, as best we know how and are able, and yell to anyone that can hear, 'WE MATTER TO EVERYONE INCLUDING TO THAT OLE CODGER THAT MADE US!'

Of Chronic Pain and Thanksgiving Dinner

I had not slept very well. The stuff of my chronic pain is constant and it awakens me at all hours including this hour at 3AM. I had spent the previous two days turkey hunting in Oklahoma and would be leaving in a few hours to fly back home. Damned chronic pain is not left behind anywhere for those who suffer with it but I had an opportunity for a change of scenery to Turkey hunt in Oklahoma and I took it just the same.

We stayed in a ranch house where there were several beds in one room and my bed was located on a wall with a number of windows. One of those windows was situated just behind my head. It would be my last night at the ranch and I looked out of the window at a dark sky lit with a trillion stars. We were far enough out of any town to where there was no light pollution and the night sky was simply magical! Knowing that this was a show I would not see in the city, I sat up, pulled on my sweats, wrapped my back tightly with my back brace, pulled on a shirt and a pair of well-worn wool socks, walked quietly across the den as to not wake anyone else, and opened the door to a world bathed in the stillness of night. A brisk breeze and the call of an owl was my welcome mat to a world of fresh air and darkness.

"Who Cooked the Goose, Who Cooked, COOKED the Goose!", the owl echoed across the forest as I walked under the cascade of a God lit sky onto a deck that overlooked a grain field. Over the years I have learned to imitate the sound of an owl during Turkey season knowing that the replication there of would help me locate a Gobbler sitting in a tree, allowing for a stalk in the dark to a location close by the weary ole bird. On this morning however, there would be no hunt, no attempting to locate a bird for a morning stalk, rather, it would provide me with a chance to sit quietly and observe the palate of stars and planets that painted the sky above me. And wow what a portrait that was painted!

Found!

The hooting of the owl echoed through the dark woods once again but then, in the middle of the night, I heard a gobble interrupting the wise ole hoot. Owls and Turkeys have a long standing war since their very creation, and more than one battle has been recorded between the two staunch enemies. Later in the morning, after coffee, I would hear 12 or 13 Gobblers respond to my own hooting but now, at 3AM, there was one ole Tom Gobbler sitting in a tree that was awake enough to challenge an owl with gobble after gobble. For the life of me, I pondered, why was that Tom awake? Here this dude was gobbling in the night air, telling the owl to keep its distance.

Just before dark, I saw the gobbler fly up into a dead Oak tree about 400 yards away and I could see him through binoculars stretch out on a limb and gobble with all of his might. Now that ole codger was still gobbling at 3AM. My thoughts rushed back to the day's previous hunts, the unsuccessful attempts to convince a weary boss gobbler that I was the sweet hen turkey he sought after, and my friend's successful crawl to take him. Unfortunately, I was reminded as well of my own painful enemy, not unlike the gobblers own nemesis the owl that just does not go away, not for a minute, an hour, nor a day, which for me is chronic pain.

At least now I could be in a different environment and hurt like a son of a gun, and in the dark of this particular night, I could sit quietly, look at the stars, and think about my time in the outdoors with Quail calling to one another and scurrying about; hawks flying across the open prairies looking for their next meal; and a new bird that will tease me into carving in the months ahead, which is the King

Scissor-tailed Flycatcher. I was able to observe one of these beautiful creations as it would sit on a barbed wire fence, fly into the field in some sort of acrobatic show, catch an insect, and come back to the barbed wire, this time 20 or 30 feet down the way from where it had previously sat. It was a masterful flight and every day I enjoyed the beautiful elegance by which it flew.

Looking up at the stars, I found myself now reflecting on my hunts and how we will reap the rewards of my successful Turkey hunt with a Thanksgiving turkey to share with my family. On a much deeper level now, while experiencing the superb handiwork of God through the star painted palate, God placed a simple question into my mind; what about Kerry's handiwork?

I sat there chilled by the morning air, looking at stars too numerous to count, listening to birds calling in the night filled woods and dwelling on the concept of Gods handiwork and now thinking about my own creative place in the star filled universe. I have a Masters of Divinity where I have spoken about God and will speak about God in a way that reflects that intentional study. I have experience as a new church planter in a number of states and have pastored some of those churches. I have been a youth minister in several churches. All of those ministerial experiences, every one of them relate to a pivotal dynamic to the call of God and that is the use of the voice and life to express the love of God as reflective of Gods ministry through the person of Jesus Christ.

The concerns of my physical condition from churches and institutions that prevent me from performing ministry in the ways I just described, have led to a deep seeded frustration in continuing ministry. Why in the world a church could not look beyond the physical limitations and see the person of Kerry Smith is beyond me. I suppose they would not give the apostle Paul a job either, what, with his own disability.

Yet now, in the dead quiet of the night, I was left pondering if the call of God can be only in the form of a professional, education filled experience or could God use the Artist Kerry Smith? It is a question and deeply spiritual wrestling match that has hounded me for a long time and then, it hit me; God Needs the Artist Kerry Smith! Underneath Gods very own star-filled creation, at 3AM, with the hoot of an owl and a gobble from a turkey I had my answer: God needs Kerry's creativity in the world!

Those on the religious right will narrowly define the roll of God's children in the universe as a singular voice to simply "win a soul for Christ." Today I will wake up, put on my braces, pull on my sweats, put on my anti-vibration gloves, and go to my shop. It is there that I will fulfill my own call of God by attempting to recreate a creation of God in the form of a bird, with the very best of my ability, with hands that don't work as well as they once did, with trifocals, with braces on my neck and back and I too will fill my place in the midst of a star-filled universe created by God.

DaVinci said it best: "Where the spirit does not work with the hand, there can be no art." That same Universe creating God has called me to create as well, imitations of what was made by God where God's Spirit will work with my very own scarred and weakened hands to fulfill God's call in my life.

Hands

They are how I communicate who I believe God to be.

Before I ever see what I am doing with my eyes, they see. I hold art pieces and feel every contour and I know if they are right. I use them in place of sand paper as I put layers of finish on wood and gunstocks, feeling the growth rings from the tree and the gentle nuances that make that tree unique. I have held the faces of my babies in them and the person who knows me better than myself. They are my hands.

Nothing is more important to an artist than their very own, creating, molding, working hands. Leonardo da Vinci said that "Where the spirit does not work with the hand, there is no art." And now, my very own hands, my God blessed, creating hands are killing me more than ever and I will see a hand specialist soon. Too soon and not soon enough.

Doctors had told me that the carpal tunnel surgery was a failure from 2 years ago and I ignored them. All the surgeries had added up to enough. And the lumbar fusion according to my pain management specialist is still at least a year from being healed totally and in his words, if ever.

Hmmm. We live in the unknowing. We believe we know. We really haven't a clue. We search for meaning in that which has no explanation.

Help! I Can't See My Face!

(Photo taken by Rebecca Webb Wilson of Hawkeye Nature Photography.)

We had sledded down a long hill in front of Nannas and Granddaddy's house on a cold, snowy day. Our son Jonathan, myself, his mom, and aunt Kristie all piled up at the end of the run. Upon finally coming to a stop in a small snow bank, completely covered in snow, Jonathan, all of about 3 years old exclaimed, "I can't see my face!"

I have discovered that even we as adults get our words and meanings all twisted. I write these words listening to it storm outside. It's 2:30 in the morning and I am having a heck of a time seeing my face. It has been a long, lonely road. Friends and family that don't know quite what to say or do, nor should they. Discrimination from potential employers for the predicament I have found myself in exists as I have tried to wrestle with my pain in a public arena only now to find out that they too follow my words as well. I had thought about deleting them but that would be as wrong as the discrimination I am facing for they reflect not just an excuse, not just a struggle, but they reflect a wrestling match between me and the almighty that eventually befriends all of humanity.

I could hide my face I suppose. Rather, what I have discovered is that, my face has been hidden like the snow that covered little Jonathans face. For if there are those who have sought to prejudge me from my words and limit their understanding of me because of the pain I wrestle with, so be it. Maybe on this day, at this dark, stormy morning, I am seeing my face and in spite of the shadow that pain has cast upon it, it is there.

After 14 years and over 21 surgeries and procedures now, I am finally managing my pain. No, not curing it, but managing it. I am firmly in agreement with Toby Keith, where he proclaims in one of his country songs, "I ain't as good as I once was, but I'm as good once, as I ever was!" Doctors had helped me with pain meds; enough to kill a freak'n cow! Scripts were written free flowing from my pain management group and when I mentioned that I was taking my pain seriously enough to manage it in other ways, I was told that it was a good thing more patients didn't do this because doctors would have no jobs. And I began to see an outline.

By the time you read this, I will have spent the day before methodically processing what I do. What I once took for granted I now have to intentionally order. I will have to manage my life consciously by what I do and don't do. I am cleaning up our garage where for years I have simply put stuff down in it, unable to bend over and place it where it belonged. It is a mess but I am cleaning it up. And when the pain comes on, instead of grabbing something from the bottle, I meditate. I begin the process of stopping the onslaught of pain and use my mind and put myself somewhere else. And then I think I see a face, a face with so much potential, so much loss, so much promise.

The fence in the yard? Needs repair. No one is going to do it and the medical bills have piled up to the place where we can't afford to have someone else to do it. It will be done a board at a time. And when I do the work, I will work for a while, and stop and meditate when the pain comes. And I see it: a face.

The rotten wood on the house? The paint has peeled off in places now and need to be replaced. The hole in my shop when the water comes through? I will repair it as well. The windows in our house? The ones that are cracked? I will fix those as well. And the birds? The birds that need finishing? The ones where when I try to complete and my hands that doctors have suggested need more cortisone and steroid shots to keep working? I will figure that out as well. And there it is; my face!

I recently have had some really good job interviews thinking that this was the fairy tale ending to my long road of pain. Jobs that would have helped us that I could do because what was required was as second nature to me as breathing. But after they have read my story, they thought differently and could not see my face. They could not see it for the veil of pain I have written about and have not understood the depth of my person. I can't help them nor anyone else see my face. But the snow has melted. I am able. I am more hopeful. I still hurt. I can now see my face.

Just A Huge Task!

The complexity of dealing with Chronic Pain Disease is as daunting as trying to pull an eagle out of this block of wood! I know it's in there. I do. But I swear, it is just an enormous task with hands that don't work like they once did and a back and neck that I still struggle with. Yet inside that block I know there is an eagle.

I have often said that Chronic Pain is a thief. It steals the physical, mental, emotional, and spiritual aspects of our person. And the great struggle is still to be. To live. Because one of the great exercises is to find tools that can carve out, carve through the pain, and release our person.

The most important tool I have in my whole shop is the knife in the picture above. It conforms to my hand and everything I have ever carved has been touched by that knife. If my shop ever burned down, this is the one tool I would attempt to salvage. To me, it is the one tool that releases the birds trapped inside of the block.

Do you know what the greatest tool is that can be used to carve out the person of Kerry Smith? Love! Unconditional, wrapped up, God like, squeeze my neck, walk with me in this stuff, Love. The same kind of love that Karen Castle Smith and Allie Smith and Jonathan Smith and close friends show!

The only way healing can ever happen to anyone, where change can happen, is to love. Never ending, tough hanging, neck hugging, walking closely, believing I am more than my pain, love.

Listening to your Life

In the midst of my own struggle with chronic pain, it requires of me a tiring, no, an exhausting work of maintaining some sense of sanity as I try to find a purpose for my suffering. I just cannot do what I once did and what it requires for me to survive is an act of constant examination and reexamination. So in the midst of this insanity, I read whatever I can find that will allow me the chance to understand my suffering.

Listening to Your Life by Frederick Buechner is a book of daily devotions whereby one reads the devotions according to the day for which they were compiled by Mr. Buechner for inspiration and guidance yet somehow I forget what day it is and thereby read the wrong day or fall behind or whatever. So today, I read the devotion for January 26 which is several weeks past. The background of this particular devotion comes from a sermon that Mr. Buechner had heard from a preacher by the name of George Buttrick.

Mr. Buechner quotes the Rev. Buttrick where he refers to the story of Jesus going to the wilderness after His baptism where he is tempted by Satan to become a kind of Messiah of great power for every segment of society. Each time Jesus declined the offer and finally delivers the news to Satan that He would become a Messiah of great humility and suffering and service and one where he would give his very life in order to take on the very sin due us in our stead. Rev. Buttrick goes on to say in his sermon that "Jesus Christ refused the crown that Satan had offered him in the wilderness but he is King nonetheless because he is crowned in the heart of the people who believe in him. And that coronation takes place among confession, and tears, and great laughter."

I read this as I find myself in the midst of dueling neurosurgeons and the song they are playing is not in tune. From Neurosurgeon A; "Mr. Smith, your fusion is not as "robust" as should be in order to remove the rods and screws and hardware that was placed there two and one half years ago as a part of your fusion surgery." (Seems that no one informed Mr. Smith that there was a better than average chance that the hardware that they would place in his back would have to be removed as a result of the pain it created. As well, no one informed Mr. Smith that about a third of all fusion surgeries result in a non-fusion union.) If Neuroguy A is correct, a twist or turn would potentially break my back creating big issues without the support of the hardware.

From Neurosurgeon B; "Mr. Smith, your fusion is just fine. We would like to go ahead with tests and if indeed the pain you are feeling in your back is from the hardware that was installed, it will require another surgery, a less invasive surgery than the initial surgery to remove the hardware. (And this surgery has its own set of risks and many who have this procedure still live in pain.)

No surgery, no procedure comes with a guarantee of reducing the pain that I live in. None of it.

In his book, Buechner focused on Buttrick's description of "great laughter", the kind in which our soul laughs out loud and sings especially when the planets are aligned and it all feels and seems right and good, a place where we usually say that we are "blessed", and therein we crown Christ as King of all! But for me, for my own stuff of life that leads to this battle with pain, where at this time it is just real heavy, it all causes me to focus on the phrase from Buttrick's words of that coronation of Christ that takes place among my own tears and not only mine, but the tears of so many that crown the living Christ King during their own struggles and tears and pain.

When I first read this line of thought, it took me a few days to wrap my head around the concept that was created by the few words Rev. Buttrick shared because that concept was just way larger than the words seem to echo.

It has all forced me to look at my pilgrimage with God, that place of the road where few travel and even fewer stay on as we journey with our own tears instead of the goodly feeling of "blessing" and it is here that I come to a crossroads as all journeys take at one time or another and that crossroads is this: at this junction of pain, and hopelessness, and sadness, at the crossroads of confession, tears, and great laughter, whom will I follow and thereby crown as King? Is it me and my own shallow understanding of the stuff of life and my own suffering that I will coronate as the King of my own existence? Or is it the one who suffered and died in my place, the one who has guaranteed a far greater future than even I could create with a pain free life?

If we walk this path, we experience a living God who holds us in our tears and laughs with us during the times of the rising tide of goodness that we interpret as blessing. And it is right here that I have figured something out. When we crown Jesus King through our tears, our confession, and our laughter, He is crowned thusly even in our great pain.

And it echoes, in this one statement, that I hope you too can hear: "Where can I go, that thou are not with me?" And would have I have ever known this unless I went to that place o

Me, Woody, and My God Forsaken Battle with Pain

The clock is ticking and I am running towards the finish line with my art project titled, "Beaver Pond Woody". Every day I get closer, though it may not look like it right now. Each step takes me to a really beautiful art piece that I will donate for a great cause. But make no mistake about it, it will always be inexorably linked to my battle with pain, and a battle it is!

I have found that pain is like an immense fire that is attempting to consume me. It is fueled not only by my genetic predisposition but by what I have learned in dealing with stress and the living of these earthly days. And every day, every hour, I am having to relearn the living of these days. Thoughts, feelings, beliefs, all are shaken as my body, mind, and soul have been placed under the microscope of pain, and I am tired. But there is no time to stop and wallow in my own stuff because this is the path my life has been placed upon. The microscope shows all kinds of stuff.

It shows thoughts, patterns, emotions, past, all sitting there, contaminating and tainting the cells of health and love and hope. And it shows the invasion that it all has had to contribute to this place where doctors interpret the self I am as in need of just one more surgery to fix whatever it is that ails me. Oh don't get me wrong; the pictures show a lot that needs afixin'. But the err of the medical community is on the side of trying to fix what they see rather than believing in the miracle of a mind and soul to heal the pain.

So I work. I am attempting to put together the pieces that will result in something special. And so to for Woody!

My One Duck Limit

It's only one. Not "one" limit. Not a half of a limit. A single drake mallard. Life just is not what it once was as an outdoorsman since my struggle with chronic pain started 13 years ago. And it definitely has made it difficult as a duck hunter. Lord knows, I do love duck hunting. Every bit of it. The smells, the anticipation, the preparation, the bonds of friendship made, the match of wits with weary greenheads, the tradition, all of it! And it is every bit that drives my wife Karen looney which is why on this day I went in the afternoon so as not to wake her too early, disrupting her work schedule(bless my heart).

So on this day, I developed a sound plan that a sound hunter would execute except I am not a sound hunter. My soundness is measured by the damned pain, the chronic pain, that I live with every single day. It is just off the charts some days and I manage it not only by pain meds but by meditation and praying and being in the outdoors when I can. It's just that this kind of being in the outdoors goes against everything one can do to manage a life with chronic pain. It's a duck hunt and duck hunting for those of us struggling with pain is like oil and water: no matter how you shake it, it still doesn't mix! To complicate matters, it had rained the night and morning before my afternoon hunt which happened to turn dirt into mud. Arkansas mud. Entrapping cement mud. I do not own an ATV which is fine because I can walk which sometimes helps if it has not rained nor if I have far to walk. But on this day I would have about mortgaged off my home for one because of the entrapment I was now experiencing because of the rain. Pull one foot up and the other one is sucked into the mud.

So what was this "sound" plan? Drive over to Arkansas from my home in Memphis and hunt in a little duck hole that has a history of hit and miss. I would pull on my waders and walk about a half a mile to my flooded rice field, lug in my wooden decoys and my Browning Maxus that I had miraculously won at a DU event(for those of you who are DU members you know what I am talking about), along with my field blind, shells, and a jacket. If you believe this was heavy, well it was, and if an alarm just started sounding in your brain that said beep, beep, beep, stupido, stupido, man with bad back have no brain, your intelligence surpasses mine which may or may not be saying much.

So I packed everything up and drove over to my duck hole which is about an hour away. Once I arrived, I got out of my truck and tried to stretch and loosen up my back. I walked around to the bed of my truck, pulled down the tail gate, pulled on my waders which is no small feat, for large feet by the way, strapped everything on, locked my truck, and started walking. About 10 steps in, I knew I was in trouble. My good friend chronic pain was now rearing its ugly head with each step and I knew I was going to have some issues. As a matter of fact, I was already planning my hot bath and ice compress on my lower back once I got home. On top of this, it was 65 degrees and I was sweating. Heck I should have worn my swimming trunks!

I really do not know what I was thinking (shut up Karen!) I cannot even lay flat in my own bed and here I was planning on lying flat in a field blind! So after my little stroll down the thick mud road, the entire road now apparently trapped on the bottom of my feet, I stood at the edge of my rice field. I threw out my decoys with my friend chronic pain, (I will call him CP for short) close in tow and bent over (CP assisted) to camouflage the layout blind. I loaded my gun, shoved my big feet, caked with Arkansas mud, into the blind, and tried to lay down flat which, by the way, is the purpose of a layout blind. What in the world was I thinking! The rods and screws and stuff from my lumbar reconstruction surgery about did me in. My surgically repaired neck was so stiff by now that I could hardly move it, and my legs and feet were killing me. I was hurting badly and I kept asking myself, am I having fun yet? I had to lay on my side and I thought, how in the heck will I ever shoot from this crazy position!

Well the ducks answered that question because there was not one to be found. They had probably headed north to colder grounds where they could regulate their temperature given how warm it had gotten to be. Ducks do not stay south if it gets warm. They will literally fly back and forth as weather dictates. After about an hour or so of this insanity, I said, okay, enough is enough. I had texted Karen, you know, the one in our family that functions with all of her faculties, and said I can't do this and I am coming home. I cannot write what she said to me.

Pushing the top of the blind off, I fought through it, pulling and working to unzip it. Then I struggled to pull my mud-caked feet out of the blind, and I slowly rose from the hell I had made. I waded out and picked up my decoys, folded up my blind, and prepared for my walk back to the truck when suddenly from the heavens, a pair of mallards circled and tried to land on top of my head! What the heck? I think they had come to laugh at me. They circled and left, naturally, after seeing a big ole slouched over, camouflaged goob standing in the middle of their sushi field!

There was only thirty minutes left in my adventure so I decided that I had already endured most of the afternoon therefore, I would stay until sunset. So I pulled my three wooden decoys out of the decoy bag, threw them out as far as I could get them and went back a few yards away from the pond close to a telephone pole that was standing close by. I called Karen and said my friend CP was kicking my butt but I was going to stay a few minutes longer. Her reply had something to do with that I had been an idiot for this long and what would a few more minutes matter to dying brain cells. No more than I had picked up the phone, unfolded it(yes it is a flip phone thank you) and gave her the news than another pair of mallards dropped out of the heavens and started circling my three decoys. I folded the phone back up, dropped it in my pocket, and gave a quick feeding chuckle on my duck call, immediately turning the ducks towards my position. They set sail, lowered their orange landing gear for a touchdown just beyond my decoys and I got ready. I picked out the drake from the pair, lifted my maxus for a moving lead, pulled the trigger and dropped him while the hen flew off.

Immediately my friend CP tapped me on the shoulder and said, you want me to go retrieve him and I thought funny; but in all reality, how in the world would I go pick him up? I sat my gun down and started the trek out to retrieve the bird with good ole CP in tow(sure do wish he would find a new friend!) By this time, I was in so much pain, I really didn't know how I was going to bend over for the retrieve.

As I approached him though, I could tell this was a mature bird. He just glowed in the rice mush! I bent over and picked him up, admiring the beauty of one of God's most beautiful creations. The iridescent green, blue, and yellow head; the rich chestnut colored chest. And the purplish, blue speculum of his wings. He was a big mature mallard drake. Only a couple of pellets had found their mark and he was perfect, absolutely perfect! Every feather was in its place. I made my way back across the field, feet sticking in mud, pain shooting with each step, but holding a really great mallard. It immediately inspired me to come back, since I carve ducks and birds for a living, and make that bird my next decorative carving project.

By the time I made it back to my telephone pole blind, it was just about time to go. I picked up my three decoys and put them in the bag, laid my one mallard on top of the decoys, and began the arduous task of dragging my butt, feet sticking in the mud, and all of my stuff, back to the truck for my trip home. By the time I strolled up to the truck, I was soaking wet from sweat, and totally engulfed with my friend CP. I strained and struggled to pull off my waders, loaded everything up and started home.

It was only one duck; one single solitary mallard drake. I was as proud of that one duck as any I had ever killed including those that had a band on their legs! I am still hurting two days later and the taste of duck hunting this season has at least temporarily been satisfied. Truthfully, I am not sure when I will go again nor am I jumping up and down to go. But for me, one duck, one simple duck, taken in a place my only son and I shared while he was growing up, taken while having to battle chronic pain, taken with decoys I made, was absolutely a gift!

My Own Cross

I had seen Red-tailed Hawks sitting on the steeple which is a cross on the top of the Second Baptist Church in Memphis, Tennessee. It would sit up there and upon seeing a squirrel scurrying on the ground, would fly down and pounce upon it for its next meal. He would use the cross for his own purposes of need. There is a bronze hawk on a cross that I created years ago that sits in a Labyrinth at Second Baptist Church and it was created from the inspiration of the actions of the Red-tailed Hawk that used the cross. When you start the walk of prayer, the hawk looks squarely at you, as if to say, this cross that I am perched on, I have used to fly from and gain my sustenance for living. What do you use the cross for?

So I celebrate Thanksgiving after driving and sleeping in a bed designed for minions, sitting in chairs designed for the flying monkeys and little people of the Wizard of Oz, and I come home and am hurting beyond anything that I have yet experienced. But I did it! I did not saddle my babies nor my wife with my pain. I will have MRI's next week in order for us to develop a plan for more surgical fun. This time, due to the scar tissue in my back from the other surgeries, I get to have what is known as a contrast MRI where they insert a dye so they can see more clearly through the rods, screws, cages, scar tissue, mole tunnels, okay not mole tunnels, but other stuff that has made my spine whatever it is. And all of this has left me really digging deep in my soul on this day because I am hurting and asking questions.

There is an image that is just real clear in the New Testament if you care to look at it and it is the image of a cross and crucifixion and a cruel death. If you are walking down a dusty road during Jesus' day, you would probably see people hanging on crosses, some dead, others dying, convicted of some sort of crime. No doubt that Jesus saw it on a regular basis and from this, he makes a statement: "whoever wishes to follow me, they must deny themselves, take up their cross, and follow me." He is saying that we should pick up a heavy piece of wood that will be nailed to the other part of the cross then stuck in the ground, and follow him. Gosh, does that whole image really get at you like it does me?

There is yet something that is deeper in this whole cross image. What Jesus describes is something reserved for criminals. Jesus is asking us to sacrifice ourselves and become a criminal for God's sake. Me a criminal for God's sake, walking around with that piece of wood tied to my arms and back, and following Jesus? There is something to this that travels yet deeper in our soul if we allow ourselves to struggle with it. It has reflections of Jesus in our society and travels the whole relationship between us and God and the world we live in. It has reflections of the scripture passage found in Micah 6:8, to do justice, love mercy, and walk humbly with our God.

But what exactly is the crime that we should commit and be given the guilty verdict for and then nailed to a cross? Our crime is found in the way we live in the world which is different than anyone else outside of the views of Jesus. Our crime is found in the way we view justice compared to the world. Our crime is how we love versus how the world loves. Our crime is found in the way we forgive. Our crime is found in the way we treat others. The world will see us as guilty and worthy of the cross when we live according to Jesus as we bear a cross.

See Jesus had this concept in his mind because he knew where he was headed. He knew that he would eventually be classified as a criminal and placed on a cross, punished for his crime, and to die a cruel death. So he asks us to do the same. He asks us to be criminals for God's sake where we have to be. He asks us to pick up the very thing that makes us human, to deny what we would really like to do with the self that we have, drag that piece of wood of our awful selves to the place where it is nailed to a beam and stuck in the ground. Earlier he had told people that to simply say Lord, Lord would not be sufficient for squat, indicating that words are hollow. Instead, he looks at us and says, deny yourself, pick up that cross that you have been given, and drag it to the place where it will be stuck in the ground and you yourself be crucified next to the son of God.

Lord have mercy because I keep trying to take that beam of wood off of my back and be something else!

So then, what is your cross? What is it that would lead you to be crucified? Karen read this and said it is real heavy. I agree. It is real heavy. What does it mean to deny myself, to pick up the cross that would lead to a crucifixion, and follow Jesus to that place? For me, the cross I bear leads me to a place where the pain I suffer and the pain others suffer needs to be seen and heard in our society that claims to have some allegiance to God in some sort of way. My cross is my pain. Pray tell, what is yours? What is it that you are dragging to the place that will lead to crucifixion?

Off the Beaten Path

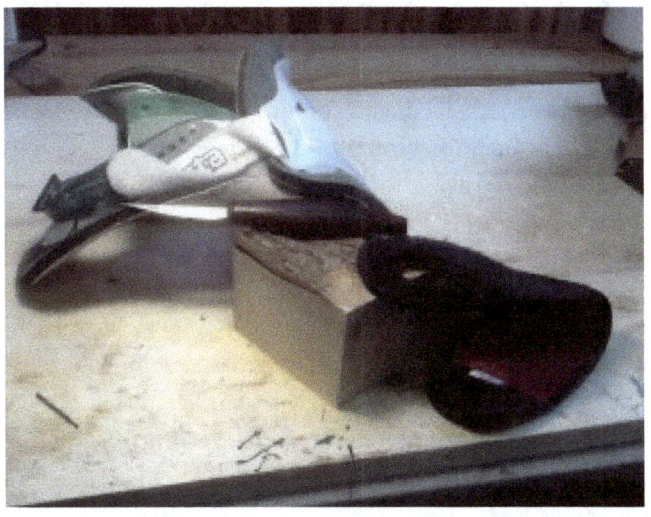

The anguish is far deeper than you can understand unless you are walking in this briar patch with me. My professional success, if I ever believed as such, was no sacrificial offering to God in order to make life easier. "My God, my God, why have you forsaken me?" Pain and anguish, no matter what we may ask for the relief of, IS a part of our existence. It is in our DNA. No matter what science does, no matter the accomplishments of our medical field, we are forsaken. We are physically incomplete, imperfect, and the masquerade ball that we have dressed up for, is all a lie. You and I will, are, shall, suffer.

Our hatred and frustration for a God we cannot grasp is commonplace throughout holy writ. When Jesus quotes the passage of scripture found in the words of David through the Psalms, while hanging on a cross, he states the same anger towards God and in the same breath, associates himself with the suffering of all of humanity. My God, My God, why have you forsaken us? Why have you taken away a touch of the heaven you reside in? Our feet and hands are pierced, and you do not hear us? Why have you left us here to suffer and die? Every one of us, from child to adult, will ask this question, and deeply struggle, as deeply as that hole I dug to remove that invasive vine, we will dig to find an answer and mostly come up clueless because we hurt.

This is precisely the place, the appointed time slot, that Jesus enters the world. This is the answer that God has given to the question of our suffering. But we want a different answer, don't we? Once again, I sit in celebration, Christmas trees and presents, pain and suffering, and am presented with this whole wrestling match with purposing my existence as some sort of a present to someone, anyone, who will walk this journey with me for you see, it is not about presents and packages but rather, it is about suffering.

The Grinch came and stole what he thought was Christmas only to find people still loving one another enough to share in their own suffering, their own humanity. It was, so to speak, the perfect community, that place called "Whoville", where everyone is tagged with a genotype of ugly faces, dumpy bodies, goofy hair, and teeth designed for beavers, but in reality, filled with love for one another.

None of it mattered though. The façade was the Grinch himself, who after experiencing betrayal and loss, after being made into the image of a villain, finally finds himself accepted. Maybe it was the stealing of the gifts that caused Whoville to wake up to the needs of the Grinch and maybe even other Grinches who lurked in the dark. Who knows the conversations that happened after the feast when the town elders stopped to ask why he would do such a thing. Maybe it took this catastrophic event of the potential loss of everything to get them to stop and say, hold on, Christmas is more. Which all leads me to the one place that recurs with every rise and setting of the sun; my own suffering.

It is not if, but when we will suffer. It is not if we will be angry with a God who we thought gave us nice fancy answers that we could wrap up in a package like those under the Christmas tree; it is when. My God, My God, why have you forsaken me, us, them? Unto us, a child is given. Unto us, us suffering flesh, made to die, made to give birth as well to suffering, laid in a manger because there is no room in any Inn, any comfortable place, because that is our purpose, our presence, our being. He will be called Immanuel, God with us. God present. In our suffering. Oh I want not to do this suffering thing. Oh how I want it to be different for all of us. I want to give a gift that is under the tree that says to all, NO MORE SUFFERING! But that is not our reality, our existence, because our existence is this; Unto us a child is given, born in a back room alley, laid in a feeding trough, who suffers with us.

Reflections of an Iris Farmer

The wait starts in February. I wonder if they are covered with enough of something to keep them from experiencing the death of winter and the damage of frost. "They" are the bulbs that will give way to some of the most beautiful flowers in God's creation known as Bearded Irises. This year is just a little different for this Iris farmer because I went throughout our yard and dug up every bulb I could find because our Bermuda grass had overtaken the bulbs that give way to the exquisite blooms.

The Bermuda grass had made a mess out of the bulbs, intertwining with the roots and in some cases squeezing the very life out of the "Jaba the Hut" looking seeds. That's what Bermuda grass does though, it invades everything and if a person has a back good enough, they will have to bend over and pull it up by the roots only to have it regain its lost advances in the given territory with more stringy runners of growth. The fact that I have a bad back is chief amongst my lawn gardener problems because I cannot bend over and pull up the runners of the Bermuda grass or for that matter in this case, protect the Iris bulbs.

My love for Irises began a number of years ago when I first saw them at "Grannie's" house, the home of wife's grandmother in Southwest Virginia. What, with me being an artist, I was enamored with the frilly blooms that sat atop the long stems coming from the bulbs. They were just magical! But my foot print into the Iris growing world was not established until years later when we bought our current home. It just so happened that, like the Bermuda grass that engulfed our flower beds, covering every living plant in our beds, so to now was the disease in my back, advancing its runners throughout my body. No matter how much the doctors pulled, which now is at 25 attempts, they have been unable to pull those damned runners up by the roots and low and behold, every so often, the nasty weed pops its ugly head up through the fertile soil and soul that is called Kerry Smith.

Realizing that I am not going to be bending over and pulling Bermuda grass, and knowing what the battle every day, I knew that if I was going to be a successful Iris breeder and farmer, I would need to change my planting method. Therefore, I dug up every iris bulb in our yard and developed a plan. I went to the local hardware store, purchased plastic cement mixing trays and planting mix, pulled out some old saw horses, sat 8 foot long boards on them and created a raised Iris bed. What they say about necessity is the mother of invention is exactly right in my case. So, I poured the dirt into the trays, gathered my bulbs, and planted them, and like a brooding hen, I have fussed over each egg, er uh, bulb.

I have thought for some time about why I am hooked on Irises. Critics will argue that they come and go just as quickly as they have burst forth with superb beauty. They just don't last long enough is what those who have them suggest. But for me, that is not the issue. For me it is much, much deeper. I mentioned earlier the comparison of Bermuda grass to my own struggle with Chronic Pain. But I wish to further explore the comparison of the growth of these flowers from the blob of matter known as a bulb and my own journey and battle with never ending pain.

If there is anything that represents our desire for newness, a new body, a new life, it is found in the yearly rebirth of our world known as Spring. If I am totally honest with myself and everyone who looks at me, as a follower of God, I would like to be set free from my body of pain. If it were not for the purpose I find in being present with my family and my love for the artistry I do, I would certainly find a way to expedite that process as many have already done who suffer with pain. If you have not understood yet, the disease of chronic pain and the disease I have been recently diagnosed with known as Adhesive Arachnoiditis, are diseases that cause unwilling participants to lose all hope, all sense of purpose, and creates immense depression. Scientists have understood for some time that in order to replicate depression in lab rats, you simply attach an electric cord to their tails and shock them indiscriminately for days on in. That is exactly what happens to we who suffer with pain. This pain is attached to us and we get shocked night and day indiscriminately.

This is why, just as from that ugly little blob known as an iris bulb comes unbelievable beauty, the ugliness of our pain suffering lives wants and needs to find beauty beyond belief. This is why I love Irises! Planted and given the right amount of love, they will bring forth beauty from the cold and death of winter and it is no less so in our lives. My belief in God tells me that resurrection happens in the midst of ugly death. The iris farmer in me knows and sees that in that ugly little bulb, extreme beauty will come forth after a cold, harsh winter. My belief in God tells me that resurrection and a new body happens after the winter of our own lives, whatever that winter may look like. This is the good news of Easter isn't it? This is the good news of we who suffer and believe in God that one day we will get a new body that does not suffer. The Irises that I love and care for remind me that no matter the ugliness I experience, beauty comes forth.

Above are some of my irises in the planters I created and yes, thanks to Nanna, I have some of Grannie's Irises in there too! May we all who suffer find ways to experience the beauty of this Spring and may it remind us that our current suffering is not the end to our painful existence!

Re-Stood

The greek word *anastasis* from which we derive the English word "resurrection" is really interesting. I am not alone in appreciating this word especially if you have lost a loved one too early or have a debilitating issue and even this day that the Lord has made has been made because of one who re-stood, relived, and revived. The word literally means to stand up again. Oh how I love that term especially knowing where my legs are going now!

Paul talked about believers who would literally stand again by the power of the resurrection if they believed in the "standing up" Christ, post death, pulled down from two sticks, transferred to a stone tomb, the two ton stone rolled away, re-standing next to God and us too someday! That's us believers, but somehow, we who have been re-stood up keep going and sitting down again. That is not what we are supposed to do if somehow we believe in the re-stood up Christ who lives right now, in the living spirit of a God who expands our existence and the universe every second, minute, hour, day, month, and year.

I battle with my own existence. I get caught up in a time that was, where I stood up because at times now, the prospect of literally re-standing after even sitting down hurts like you wouldn't believe. The faith that we hold on to tells us however that one day, we will again stand, risen, new legs and the whole bit.

Sometimes movies tell the story of our Christian faith in ways that we have to use our minds to dig in to. So, the movie "Avatar" depicts a guy who is a paraplegic who cannot stand and through the use of a fictional being, gets new legs; gets to run, dig his toes in the cool moist dirt, and look up into the sun and laugh. He gets re-stood on new legs.

We are literally re-stood in this life because of our belief, asked to go forward, with new legs, not backwards, with whatever in the heck we have that may or may not work. Forward. Re-stood. Misunderstood at times because the love we are asked to carry and walk with. Mind, fractured body; faith, yet again, found not in whatever we don't have but in someone who lived and died and stood again who asks us to do the same. It is the day the Lord has made, rejoicing most of all because, on this day, he and we will be re-stood, raised again, out of the tomb and ground, and even poured into the mason jar for Pete's sake!

Forward.

Still Struggling for Release

Six years ago I created the bronze sculpture shown above after having a Spinal Cord Simulator implanted to help me control my chronic pain. It was supposed to last 7-10 years. It lasted 4. I sat up all night one night right after that surgery as I struggled to find release of my own pain.

It was first made out of clay and then it was bronzed using the lost wax method. The bronze depicts a dove, struggling, pulling to find release from the muck of stuff that was entrapping the bird of peace. It described on a deeper level my own desire for release from pain.

Yesterday I started with another pain management specialist to find new ways of managing my pain. I have had 4 of them, each one working on another piece of the Kerry Smith puzzle. As the doctor finished combing through the pages of my file, he closed it and said, "you, my friend, have been through it!" I wanted to say, "Duh!"

We then began discussions concerning the government regulatory board clamp down that is happening on narcotic pain Meds because of abuse. He then said to me, "For someone who has gone through as much as you, we will use any means necessary to help you manage your pain. Let's work together to see what we can do!"

You must understand the weight that was lifted off of my shoulders upon hearing his words! I have had doctors and clinics to change my medication arbitrarily not because of my need but because of external pressure. No message, no nothing, just whammy, medicine diminished or stopped without a word. Now finally, here was a doctor who understood and did not start with his own conclusions, but rather with what I actually needed!

This is but one ongoing battle that exists for those who suffer with chronic pain. To be heard, to have my needs met, to be seen as a human being, worthy of getting fixed rather than a cash cow for the medical profession is such a breath of fresh air. He was truly a beacon in my storm, as I still struggle for Release

The Day the Lord Has Made?

In the picture above, I am standing next to one of my creations, a hawk on a cross that is a part of a Labyrinth at Second Baptist Church in Memphis, Tennessee. Why of all things would I put a hawk on a cross?

The top of the steeple at this particular church has a cross. One Spring, a pair of hawks who nested in a tall oak tree near the steeple, would use that cross as a launching point to dive bomb their prey. We witnessed a decline of squirrels during that year as the hawks claimed their prize from the cross.

If you stand at the beginning of the prayer walk where my hawk and cross are installed, the hawk faces you. I think it asks us a question: "What do you do with this cross that I use to gain an advantage on the prey I'm pursuing?"

C. Kerry Smith

I write this post on what is supposed to be "the day that The Lord has made!" 116 million Americans will suffer with chronic pain on "the day that The Lord has made" and not darken the doors of buildings that claim such due to a difficult access and pews so hard that our forefathers created them thusly hoping to prevent attenders from falling asleep due to dull sermons. (They also needed men with long poles that stood at the back of the church to gently nudge a snoozer back awake should they fall comatose during the reverends dull sermon!)

By all accounts, 80% of America will not darken the doors of the church that proclaims "this is the day that The Lord has made" of which I will be but one. As one who suffers from chronic pain, who lives life an hour, sometimes a minute at a time, I ask today the same question my hawk asks: to what advantage or lack thereof do you/me/us use the cross, the symbol of pain, suffering, and redemption?

The Gift

I write this morning to the sights and sounds of a squirrel having been traumatized by a Cooper's Hawk who tried to have him for breakfast. He is now sprawled out on the side of an oak tree, tail quivering and barking at a bird of prey that almost ended his life. The young hawk, clothed in the kind of feathers that represent an immature bird, after unsuccessfully obtaining breakfast, came and sat about 20 feet from me, right after the sun had risen, unaware that I was so close.

They are called "Thin Places" in the Celtic tradition of spirituality. A "Thin Place" is where the veil that separates heaven and earth is lifted and one is able to receive a glimpse of the glory of God. Just now was one of those places. Another is from my most recent visit with my pain doctor and I wanted to share that particular thinning space. There is a Celtic saying that "heaven and earth are only three feet apart, but in the thin places that distance is even smaller!" I had returned home from an appointment with my pain doctor, parked my truck, and reached over in to the passenger seat to gather whatever paperwork and stuff the doctor had given me before exiting my truck.

The appointment had gone well for the most part. I had brought with me on this day an article that had been written about my pain struggle and my portfolio of previous art pieces. As a side note, I want you to understand that I look at my portfolio with a strong sense of sadness. It represents a time when I could sit in my shop and work endlessly with little or no pain as I completed the beautiful art projects represented in the pages of this book. This time for artists is called a "zone", where an artist can sit in one place and mentally and spiritually go to another place that allows for greater creativity. My pain often prevents me from going to that "zone", unable to stand after a few minutes of work or unable to focus on the project.

I had taken the portfolio to allow the doctor to see what it was that was at stake in my work with him and he was so very much impressed. The pictures reflected not only just fancy art pieces but it reflected a gift that I have always acknowledged to be straight from the living God, pictures of thin places represented through my creations. And now the gift if not gone, is certainly leaving quickly. For you see, I go to my shop and it now becomes more difficult than ever due to the pain and shortness of time by which I am able to do what I have loved. Am I depressed? Oh yeah! More depressed than I can express to anyone who reads this. I have watched my life as it has grown more limiting in what I can do and I keep yelling to the God of gifts, please pull me off of this ride, please! Please help me to continue in those precious thin places!

After getting home and pulling into the driveway, I got out of the truck and looked down and low and behold there it was; a feather. I had no room in my hands to pick it up so I went inside, threw my belongings down and returned to its resting place. I bent over and picked it up, holding it in my hand, and I knew exactly who it had belonged to; it was from a Cooper's Hawk. It was a primary feather, the feather found on the outer part of a wing which gave the swift flying bird the ability to do what God had empowered it to do. I held the feather by the quill and stroked the hair-like fibers, going first against the flow and then grooming the hairs back in place. This was not just a simple feather my friends, It was and is a thin place.

One of the topics that I am grappling with is how do I continue to create. The pain has all taken its toll. The surgeries have all taken their toll. The depression has taken its toll. And here in lies the beauty of a simple molted feather. It is that time of the year when birds are molting and getting prepared for what the next season lies ahead. If it is waterfowl or songbirds, they are being prepared to fly the distances needed and the strength for the fall and winter through the shedding of old feathers for new ones. If it is a bird of prey, it is dropping old feathers and growing new ones that will help it to be able to fly and attack whatever is needed for sustenance, able to do and be what God has created it to be.

So how do I know that this is the feather from a Cooper's Hawk? A few years ago I carved and painted a flying Cooper's Hawk that I titled "Amazing Grace".

I had been inspired to do the carving as I observed a Cooper's Hawk on the grounds of the church where my family and I were attending. I was in the midst of one of those "life transitions" and was asking God for a little bit of clarification. In the midst of this all, I became a constant observer of this Cooper's Hawk and even named her Grace. I watched her dive and chase songbirds and squirrels, sometimes successful, most times not, but the whole of the events of this time, throughout the weeks and months of watching her, was nothing other than a spectacular "Thin Place", the space that God had given to me where the veil was lifted and I was able to experience the glory of God.

Now, instead of the bird, instead of watching and being inspired by the acrobatics of a beautiful raptor, I was holding a molted feather from its wing. Suddenly for me, the thin place became a little thinner and the veil between dirt and spirit, between suffering and rest, between heaven and earth was ever so slightly lifted. My pain doctor, I am convinced, is a gift straight from God. Over the last three months, I have "molted" the levels of narcotic pain meds, molted some attitudes regarding my pain, suffered less, become more hopeful, found new treatment options, found a new pain counselor, discovered more possibilities for treatment, started vitamin supplements, taken more control of my pain management and am feeling less disabled. Am I cured? Oh heck no. Do I have less pain? By all means! Do I wrestle with all that lay in front of me? Yes! But at least now I am on a journey that I am able to see and experience good options for treatment and maybe even a molting of old flight feathers for new ones.

The Yoke and a Different Kind of Labor Day

(Photo by Carmen Anderson.)

The day had started like most days. The morning sun was beating down on the dusty dirt road and little rain was in sight. The days were now beginning to get a little shorter and the heat had started to be less oppressive. Summer was now turning to fall and the grain fields were ripe for harvest. Jesus could look out and see the fruits of the labor of the farmer. He knew the farming routine like the back of his hand even though his trade was with wood. He had seen the drama play out for as long as he could remember.

The two oxen were given the yoke and it was no easy chore to even place it over their heads, settling it onto the base of their neck and their shoulders. Gosh how stubborn those huge animals were! It was quite an event to get them to plow along the path the farmer wanted. Sometimes the hard headed oxen listened; at other times they would need a good hard directive to keep them on their path with a wooden stick that had a nail in it.

Jesus was standing in the shadows of a place of worship watching as the Pharisees and Sadducees entered into the synagogue while looking just across the fields at the laborers cutting the wheat for harvest. Some could go into the house of the Lord while others were left standing. Jesus was watching the whole scene play out. Between the farmer and the farm hands working in the field, the "holy" men entering the synagogue, and the outcasts unable to read or hear the word of God, a crisis was about to occur like a car stuck on a train track with the conductor blowing the horn from the engine of a fast moving train. It was coming by golly!

Oh how heavy, how burdensome it all was, he thought. Those people entering that synagogue with all of those rules; how could a person stand to walk with the heavy yoke of a religion draped over their heads like a heavy yoke, being yanked around by the straps of a hard headed religious know-it-all, and the pull of a translated religion based on heavy laws and opinions that over time would wear a person completely down; Is this what the love of God was supposed to be about, he thought?

Between the crossroads of this religious place and a grain field ripe for harvest, it hit him: this whole event is exactly how people believe they should relate to God. The do's and don'ts, the regulations, all of it, every single word of it that those leaders required, all, painted a picture of a God of wrath and judgment and ritual. If there was one thing, one thing Jesus knew, it was that this kind of ritual did not represent who He knew God to be. In the shadows of the holy place, within earshot of a farmer's toil and labor, of fancy Pharisees prancing around in their religious garb, and people on the outside looking in, he began to speak:

"I praise you, Father, Lord of heaven and earth, because you have hidden these things from the wise and learned, and revealed them to little children. Yes, Father, for this is what you were pleased to do.

"All things have been committed to me by my Father. No one knows the Son except the Father, and no one knows the Father except the Son and those to whom the Son chooses to reveal him.

"Come to me, all you who are weary and burdened, and I will give you rest. Take my yoke upon you and learn from me, for I am gentle and humble in heart, and you will find rest for your souls. For my yoke is easy and my burden is light."

People who heard those words of Jesus, his disciples, the outcasts, and the hyper religious knew what Jesus was saying. The "sinners", those who were not allowed into the holy place, knew the heavy yoke of both the ox and the religion that played out every day. If you were on the outside of the religion of the day, you knew it was impossible to keep all the do's and don'ts.

He finished his sermon and immediately allowed his life's events to be a living kind of illustration where once again, he would tick off a bunch of those he would call hypocrites, the same bunch that would kill him one day. He would take his disciples after the farmer had finished his work and walk through the field, picking and eating whatever grain they could find on the day of the Lord. Problem was that it was the Sabbath, and Jesus had a point to make, a point that would only further to anger the Pharisees that while they were wearing people out with their laws, they had neglected the point of any religion which was mercy and justice and a relieving of heavy burdens in the lives of people who hurt.

No more had Jesus began to walk through the field than the Pharisees, who were watching from their building, yelled out, "Look! Your disciples are doing what is unlawful on the Sabbath." Jesus, having heard their religious baloney all too many times before had an idea what they were going to say.

Jesus yelled back to them, "Haven't you read what David did when he and his companions were hungry? He entered the house of God, and he and his companions ate the consecrated bread—which was not lawful for them to do, but only for the priests. Or haven't you read in the Law that the priests on Sabbath duty in the temple desecrate the Sabbath and yet are innocent? I tell you that something greater than the temple is here. If you had known what these words mean, 'I desire mercy, not sacrifice,' you would not have condemned the innocent. For the Son of Man is Lord of the Sabbath."

Oh it was on now! They knew their Bible well enough to know that no man born from a woman was going to be THEIR Messiah! They were sure of what the Bible said, dead set sure, and no one was going to misinterpret what they felt was right to do by the good book! And to say that there was "something greater than the temple?" Really?

To make a point of what he meant by how they were using their temple, he upped the ante with one more little exercise to prove his point. He healed a man, on the Lord's day, in the temple of the most high and kinda hit them with their own Bible from 1 Samuel 15:22 that reads; "Does the LORD delight in burnt offerings and sacrifices as much as in obeying the LORD? To obey is better than sacrifice, and to heed is better than the fat of rams."

But if you had known what this means, 'I DESIRE COMPASSION, AND NOT A SACRIFICE,' you would not have condemned the innocent. 8"For the Son of Man is Lord of the Sabbath."

Found!

Something greater than the house of the Lord? Compassion, not worship? People over the law?

Happy Labor Day!

What Do We Do with It?

Life is not just what we are but rather what we make of it. I am a daddy not just because of the title and the events where two people came into existence. I am a daddy because of what I do with that gift.

I am a husband of a phenomenal person not just because of that one special day of flowers and cake and blessings but because of how much I love that person and what I do with that gift.

I laid in bed trying to make sense of it all. That was 12 years ago and it still makes no sense. I could hold a knife, a burning tool, and a brush. Not for very long though but I could hold it. The pain touched and overrode everything everywhere. The opiates, the meditation, the prayers, relationships, jobs, vacations, travel, everything. Everything that is but one place: the place where I could escape and transcend my pain through creating the little teal in the caption above.

It was a Christmas present in 2001 to Karen. I had ruptured two discs in my lumbar area. I drug my left leg around in immense pain. It was the start of my life with pain and I can honestly say that there has not been one day when I haven't been in pain. But I laid in bed and created the little green winged teal for Karen, wood chips on my chest while the dogs of pain I kept at bay. And in creating that bird, I found a gift that has helped me exist in the midst of mind blowing pain. I learned that I could escape my pain by doing my art work.

But I learned something way more significant on a much deeper level and it is this:

Life is not just what we are but rather what we make of it

What to Make of this Mess

I am not sure what to make of it, this, this, pronouncement or whatever it was by my neurosurgeon this week. I have read for quite some time the dangers of opening Pandora's box or in this case "Kerry's box" the number of times it and I have been opened. It's just a danged lot people and I am trying to go back now and retrace my footsteps as to what led me to my decisions and if I am not careful, I can get to kicking myself something awful.

We inherently trust a valued medical profession. The results of my surgeries have even baffled my surgeons with one saying to me some 6 weeks after one particular surgery, "Do you mean to tell me that my surgery did not help you?"

You must understand what is at stake during this time. I was declared disabled the first time of my application process, and that was partly due to the staffer in the disability office looking at my case and literally calling me every few weeks to urge me to complete the paper work for disability. On the one hand, I am so disabled. It has all now impacted me to the place where there are few places on my body that do not hurt. But do I think of myself as disabled? Heck no! I often find myself as a spectator to my own body. It is like I am watching a wrestling match between the warring factions under my skin.

Yet it is not just the physical war; It is the mental, spiritual, emotional, social, and everything underneath the skin kind of war. To sit down and get into a zone for an artist, to the complexity of the detailing work that I do is now fleeting because of the sheer magnitude of it all. I could picture being some old guy sitting around a fire at the ripe ole age of 90, way in the winter of life, whittling and carving. But not at 50 something. I am too freaking young for this ya'll!

No, I am not dying and I have some friends who are dying and they now look at a period to the sentence of a life God has given them here on earth. I suppose a period may be worthwhile, a blessing so to speak, an end to the suffering a person is going through. See I am not sure when this will stop nor do any of the doctors I am seeing. They just don't know. No one knows which is where I am. The only thing, the only thing I know is that I live in pain. I sleep in pain. I used to be able to sit down at my work bench and enter a place that is untouched by pain. That time is no longer and I now do my artistry in pain if I can do it at all. The pictures of my art work I cherish! I love to hunt and fish, but now those places are filled with pain. Sitting, standing, lying, all of it, in pain. The pain meds that they have prescribed me now have affected my digestive track so look soon for me to write something about trying medical marijuana. Oh, and that too has some issues. See, each month, I have to give a urine sample and if I have traces of anything in my blood stream that they have not prescribed me, they can stop seeing me as well as any other doctor and I am done with any kind of pain meds. So, once I try Medical Marijuana in the great state of Tennessee, given that it is illegal, I am done with the professional pain treatment option. Damned if I do; damned if I don't!

Why am I writing this? No this is not my attempt to find pity for what I am going through. That boat sailed a long time ago. I could just as soon ride this internal horse off into the private sunset. I could privatize what I am going through but see, all those years ago, when I decided to live a life with some type of ownership given to a God far bigger than me, I gave up a really big part of me and that is navigation. And so do any of us when we chose to follow the likes of a God who came and lived life quite publicly. We give up navigation or rather should give up navigation. Our personal compass that we assume can get us from point a to point b is off. The directions meaningless. The maps eschewed. All direction is wrong for living life the way our society says we should live life if indeed we have come to follow a traveling carpenter oriented towards another world.

I have to finish this because, my hands are hurting. My neck is hurting. My head is hurting. My eyes are hurting. My back is hurting. My hips are hurting. My legs are hurting. My feet are hurting. And my heart and spirit and mind are hurting even more because my babies and the woman I love deserve better. At times, so does my world. But friends, I conclude with this one thought. I am not God. I sometimes think that I am. Or at least act like it. But I am not.

Tonight I watched a show on the Discovery Channel about the Hubble Telescope and was reminded about my place in the universe. The number of planets and stars are beyond our comprehension and the more we see, the more there is to see. It is infinite and beyond our scope of reason. Because I cannot see those planets and stars does not mean they do not exist. I just can't see them. And if in my pain and suffering I have come to understand anything, it is this: because I cannot figure this out, because I cannot find an answer to this suffering does not mitigate for one moment the love of family and friends nor does it cover up the love of a God I cannot see neither does it take away my capacity to love and express love. And for these things, for these things I would never have come to understand unless I went through this pain, for that, I am grateful beyond words.

Oh, Heck yeah, you *ARE* worth a lot!

(The title of the above sculpture is Embracing the Journey. It is located at the Baptist Reynolds Hospice House in Collierville, TN. The sculpture represents that at the time of our death and the release of our suffering, God lifts us up and embraces us at our journeys end.)

Our day had ended like most. Karen came home and found me in bed. For me, it had all now taken a dark turn and I contemplated how best and easiest to end my life. Gone was my artistry because my hands could not hold the tools of my trade. Gone was my identity as a minister because one church after another looked at my disability rather than my ability. Gone were my strong physical attributes that could move a mountain. Gone was my ability to live in the outdoors in the way I wanted. Gone was normalcy in life due to the constant pain I was in. Gone now, I believed, was God.

She pulled into the driveway, stepped out of her car, walked up the sidewalk and through the front door, received the nightly greeting from our dachshund, paraded herself right into the bedroom and sat on the side of the bed and asked me, "Are you suicidal?" I began to cry and I was totally honest with her; 'Yes, I am', and with the answer came the tears. Not only did my tears fall, but so did Karen's. We have been through a lot and have had some great experiences. Chronic pain however has been an unwelcome invasive species in our existence. There is literally no place that pain has not touched. Vacations have been canceled, medical bills have piled up, and loneliness has crept in to become an unwelcome friend to both of us. She has learned to read me now after all of these years and she was spot on.

The conversation turned quickly to things that I actually could do rather than what I could not do and to our future rather than the present. Grandbabies that would need a lap to crawl in and last time I looked, it had become an unwelcome physical trait. Ears to hear of the difficulties of adult-becoming that my children are going through that are still usable . A role to play in a few weddings someday, even if it meant having my rear end hauled down the center isle of a church in a red western flyer wagon! Meals that I have become a master of preparing that gave her a little more palate to endure her own precious yet stress filled life. Flowers that I could still arrange in a planter, though more slowly and painfully than before, that had become life giving to her. I could still do a small amount of my art work, no, not mass production, but something at least that could identify God as a God of beauty and love. Words that I was now beginning to learn to put together in a highly creative format where people gain help for their own struggles were beginning to be read.

They were all pieces, every one of them. Scattered pieces, like that of a jigsaw puzzle. They are the pieces of my life that to Karen had far more value to her than I had thought. And at that very moment, I determined one thing, one very important thing; the pieces of Kerry Smith were worth more to my people and to my world and maybe to my God than none of Kerry Smith. In my contemplation of suicide, I was therefore making none of Kerry Smith available to no one or no thing but earth worms, I suppose.

Would I be cured? I don't know, but if I ended my life I may never find out! Would I still have pain? Probably, possibly, heck, I really could not know definitely. Would my life be as it once was? No. Could it still be life, yes!

It was at this point, in the crossroads of my own crisis, a book was suggested by a dear friend who from a distance walks with me in this pain manure. The title is, "Man's

Search for Meaning" by Viktor Frankl. Viktor was a concentration camp survivor and if you have not read the book, you need to, because if someone found a way to survive a concentration camp, I am thinking his tools could fit into our own tool chest.

In this book, Viktor discusses why it was that some people were surviving the concentration camp he was placed in and why some of them were not. His conclusion, after watching poor souls who were the shadows of their previous selves, was that if a concentration camp prisoner had some reason for living, something that pulled them forward, they would survive. He gave story after story of prisoners who died for no other reason than they had lost a reason to live. Those that survived, even if their reason for existing was misplaced or misappropriated to some area, would find a way to survive. His own personal reason for living was the belief that one day he would see his wife again even though in reality, she was already dead. He had no way of knowing, but he believed and imagined that one day he would see her outside of the prison fences.

Chronic pain patients are similar to prisoners. They are bound by a body that no longer works as it once did and they are prisoners inside of that jail cell. Often they feel that there is no other way to escape than to end their lives. Chronic pain patients are twice as likely to commit suicide as the average population according to Judy Foreman in her book, "A Nation in Pain". If you are suffering from chronic pain, you know this fact deep down, don't you? Life is not what it once was and you struggle to find a new meaning for living. Friends don't understand. Family, to a great degree, does not totally get it. Your purpose and reason for living the life that you once lived has now gone.

Ask yourself this question; Are the pieces of your life worth more to the world we live in, than none of your life? To a child learning to read, can you teach them how to read? To a wife or husband attempting to understand what you are going through and giving their all, can you prepare lasagna? To a darkened world, can you create something of beauty? And out of your own pain manure, can you plant flowers? The pieces of your life, those now scattered about, those incomplete pieces, are worth more to your loved ones, to your God, to your world, than none of you. Chronic pain may have clouded the lenses of how you see your life, but know one thing; your life is far more valuable than you realize!

Hear the words of Jesus as found in Matthew 5 starting in verse 1:

> *1Now when Jesus saw the crowds, he went up on a mountainside and sat down. His disciples came to him, 2and he began to teach them*
>
> *He said:*
>
> *3 "Blessed are the poor in spirit, for theirs is the kingdom of heaven.*
>
> *4Blessed are those who mourn, for they will be comforted.*
>
> *5Blessed are the meek, for they will inherit the earth.*
>
> *6Blessed are those who hunger and thirst for righteousness, for they will be filled.*
>
> *7Blessed are the merciful, for they will be shown mercy.*
>
> *8Blessed are the pure in heart, for they will see God.*
>
> *9Blessed are the peacemakers, for they will be called children of God.*

10Blessed are those who are persecuted because of righteousness, for theirs is the kingdom of heaven.

11 "Blessed are you when people insult you, persecute you and falsely say all kinds of evil against you because of me.

12Rejoice and be glad, because great is your reward in heaven, for in the same way they persecuted the prophets who were before you.

13 "You are the salt of the earth. But if the salt loses its saltiness, how can it be made salty again? It is no longer good for anything, except to be thrown out and trampled underfoot.

14 "You are the light of the world. A town built on a hill cannot be hidden.

15Neither do people light a lamp and put it under a bowl. Instead they put it on its stand, and it gives light to everyone in the house.

16In the same way, let your light shine before others, that they may see your good deeds and glorify your Father in heaven.

www.ingramcontent.com/pod-product-compliance
Lightning Source LLC
Chambersburg PA
CBHW071526080526
44588CB00011B/1573